Writing Short Words and Sentences

in Cursive for Elementary Kids

Book 3

HAVING FUN CURSIVE WRITING WITH BLYTHE

Dr. Melissa Caudle

Absolute Author
Publishing House

CHILDREN'S DIVISION

Dedicated to all of my grandchildren.

Writing Short Words and Sentences in Cursive for Elementary Kids
Copyright 2020
Dr. Melissa Caudle

Publisher: Absolute Author Publishing House
Editor: Dr. Carol Michaels
Cover Designer: MD. Sheikh Shoeb Uddin
Illustrator: Sidra Ayyaz

ISBN: 978-1-951028-79-4

1. Education   2. English as a Second Language   3. Handwriting

Dear Parents and Teachers:

Congratulations! You want your children to master cursive writing and they have progressed through the first two books in this series. Now it is time to put it all together and apply what they have learned.

I have outlined this book strategically for children to use similar learning movements to master cursive writing. It begins by writing single words, then progresses to writing complete sentences.

I carefully constructed this series of workbooks using sound principles of teaching. Each child must have completed the firsts two books in this series and practice daily. Like most skills learned in life, it takes practice. It is no different when it comes to cursive writing. That is why I recommend Book 4 in this series, *Lined Cursive Writing Practice Book,* for his or her additional practice.

This cursive handwriting book series is divided into four books.

- Book 1 – *Tracing and Writing the Cursive Alphabet in Lower and Uppercase from A – Z*
- Book 2 – *Cursive Writing Numbers, Colors, Seasons, Months, and Names*
- **Book 3 – *Writing Short Words and Sentences in Cursive***
- Book 4 - *Lined Cursive Writing Practice Book*

In this book, children will use the skills learned in books 1 and 2 to write short words and sentences in cursive. Be sure to have them warm up by tracing over each upper and lowercase alphabet. Likewise, as you introduce them to short words and sentences, have them follow the arrow-numbered tracing pattern, see below, several times before they progress to tracing the dotted words, and then complete the independent practice.

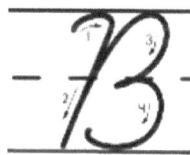

Supplies Needed:

#2 Pencil

Eraser

Pencil Sharpener

TIPS FOR PARENTS

1. When working with your child, monitor their progress, and demonstrate how to trace the letters and then to write them. Children learn by watching.

2. Make sure there is sufficient light in the area.

3. Always use the lined cursive paper when instructing your child. It is challenging for them to use unlined paper or regular lined paper used in school. It is wise to invest in my Book 5 *Lined Cursive Writing Practice Book* to provide your child with plenty of space to practice writing in cursive.

4. Make sure that your child is sitting at a table or desk where they can comfortably write and have excellent posture. It is okay if your child wants to move their paper diagonally to create a slant for writing. It is the most natural way. For right-handed children, the paper should be parallel with the child's hand slanted left at about a twenty percent angle. If you have a left-handed child, they will slant their paper to the right. The essential factor is that they are comfortable.

Happy cursive writing,

Dr. Melissa Caudle

Are you ready to learn how to write complete sentences in cursive? Let's go!

UPPERCASE CURSIVE ALPHABET

Review the uppercase cursive alphabet by tracing the numbered arrows.

A B C D E F G H I J K L M N O P Q R S T U V W Y X Z

$\mathcal{A}$ — $\mathcal{B}$ — $\mathcal{C}$ — $\mathcal{D}$

$\mathcal{E}$ — $\mathcal{F}$ — $\mathcal{G}$ — $\mathcal{H}$

$\mathcal{I}$ — $\mathcal{J}$ — $\mathcal{K}$ — $\mathcal{L}$

$\mathcal{M}$ — $\mathcal{N}$ — $\mathcal{O}$ — $\mathcal{P}$

$\mathcal{Q}$ — $\mathcal{R}$ — $\mathcal{S}$ — $\mathcal{T}$

$\mathcal{U}$ — $\mathcal{V}$ — $\mathcal{W}$ — $\mathcal{X}$

$\mathcal{Y}$ — $\mathcal{Z}$

LOWERCASE CURSIVE ALPHABET

Review the lowercase alphabet by tracing over the numbered arrows.

A B C D E F G H I J K L M N O P Q R S T U V W Y X Z

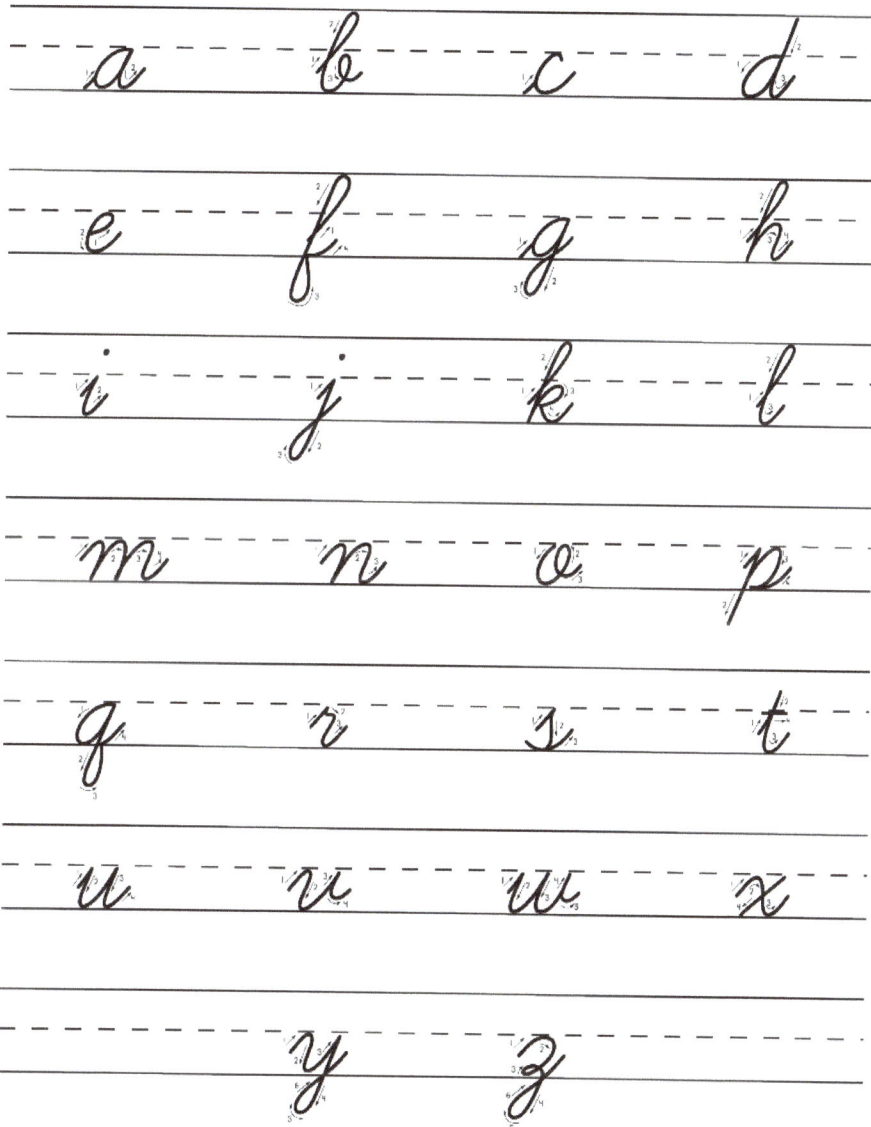

a *b* *c* *d*

e *f* *g* *h*

i *j* *k* *l*

m *n* *o* *p*

q *r* *s* *t*

u *v* *w* *x*

y *z*

That was great!

Are you ready to learn how to write short words in cursive? Take your time tracing each word by following the numbered arrows. Ready? Set. Go!

Apple   apple

Apple

apple

Bee   bee

Bee

bee

Cake

cake

Cake

cake

Dog

dog

Dog

dog

Eel   eel

Eel

eel

Frog   frog

Frog

frog

Gate   *gate*

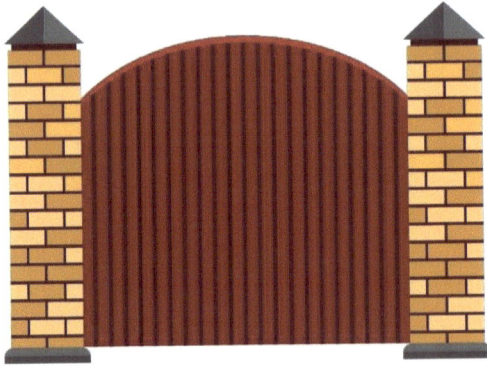

Gate

gate

Happy   *happy*

Happy

happy

Igloo

igloo

Igloo

igloo

Jump

jump

Jump

jump

Kite

kite

Kite

kite

Lime

lime

Lime

lime

Milk　　　*milk*

Milk

milk

Net　　　*net*

Net

net

Ocean

ocean

Ocean

ocean

Pie

pie

Pie

pie

Quail

Quail *quail*

Quail

quail

Rooster

Rooster *rooster*

Rooster

rooster

Sun $^{2}_{1}$ ^{3} sun $^{2}_{1}$ $^{1}_{2}$ ^{3}

Sun

sun

Tent ^{1} $^{2}_{1}$ $^{1}_{2}$ ^{1} $^{4}_{3}$ tent $^{2}_{1}$ ^{4} $^{1}_{2}$ $^{1}_{2}$ $^{4}_{3}$

Tent

tent

Umbrella   umbrella

Umbrella

umbrella

Vase   vase

Vase

vase

Whale

whale

Whale

whale

X-ray

x - ray

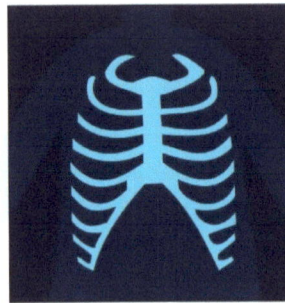

X-ray

x-ray

Yolk *yolk*

Yolk

yolk

Zoo *Zoo*

ZOO

Zoo

Zoo

You did great!

Are you ready to learn how to write short sentences in cursive? Remember to follow the numbered arrows. **Ready? Set. Go!**

The red apple is pretty.

The red apple is pretty.

The bee is black and yellow.

The bee is black and yellow.

Mom baked me a cake.

Mom baked me a cake.

Two pink flowers bloomed.

Two pink flowers bloomed.

It snows in the winter.

It snows in the winter.

I love to swim in the summer.

I love to swim in the summer.

Ava and Emily love purple.

Ava and Emily love purple.

Carter and Roger play ball.

Carter and Roger play ball.

School starts in August.

School starts in August.

I have one brown dog.

I have one brown dog.

I have two orange cats.

I have two orange cats.

The green frog jumps funny.

The green frog jumps funny.

I like cherry pie.

I like cherry pie.

When I am happy, I smile.

When I am happy, I smile.

The rooster crows.

The rooster crows.

The igloo is made of ice.

The igloo is made of ice.

I like camping in a tent.

I like camping in a tent.

The kite has many colors.

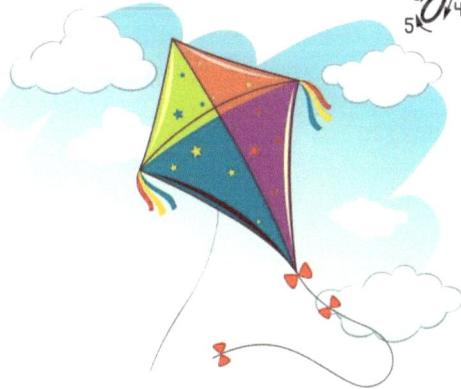

The kite has many colors.

The whale is very large.

The whale is very large.

The zoo is a fun place to visit.

The zoo is a fun place to visit.

Flowers bloom in the spring.

Flowers bloom in the spring.

Ice cream is frozen.

Ice cream is frozen.

I love to eat pizza.

I love to eat pizza.

I like to play in the park.

I like to play in the park.

OTHER BOOKS IN THE SERIES

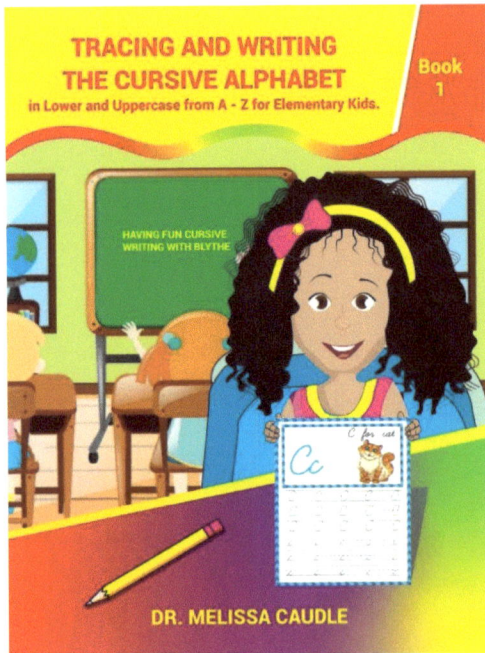

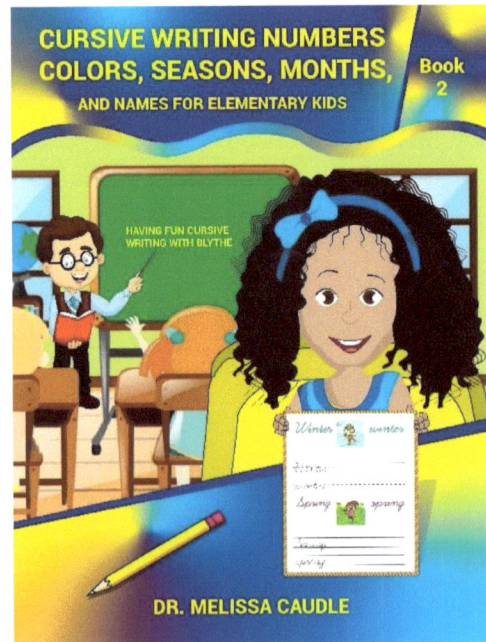

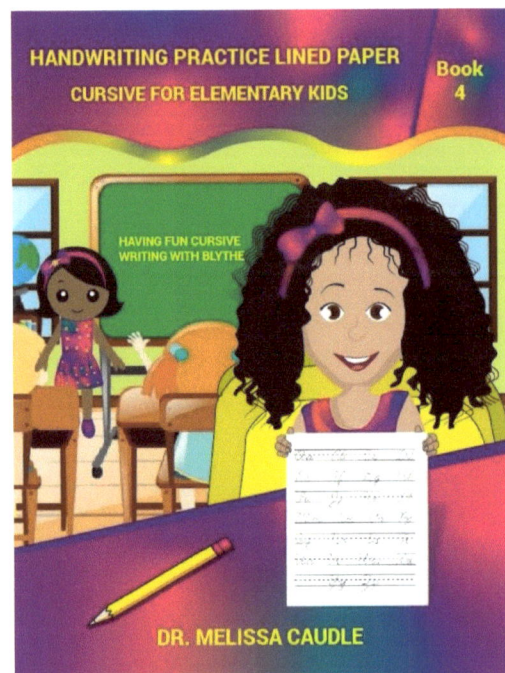

TRACING AND WRITING THE CURSIVE ALPHABET
in Lower and Uppercase from A - Z for Elementary Kids.

Book 1

HAVING FUN CURSIVE WRITING WITH BLYTHE

DR. MELISSA CAUDLE

CURSIVE WRITING NUMBERS COLORS, SEASONS, MONTHS, AND NAMES FOR ELEMENTARY KIDS

Book 2

HAVING FUN CURSIVE WRITING WITH BLYTHE

DR. MELISSA CAUDLE

WRITING SHORT WORDS AND SENTENCES IN
CURSIVE FOR ELEMENTARY KIDS

Book 3

HAVING FUN CURSIVE WRITING WITH BLYTHE

DR. MELISSA CAUDLE

HANDWRITING PRACTICE LINED PAPER
CURSIVE FOR ELEMENTARY KIDS

Book 4

HAVING FUN CURSIVE WRITING WITH BLYTHE

DR. MELISSA CAUDLE

LEARN CURSIVE WRITING FOR TEENS

From A-Z Using Leadership Quotes

- Uppercase
- Lowercase
- Short Words
- Short Sentences

Dr. Melissa Caudle

LEARNING CURSIVE WRITING
for Young Adults

USING WORDS TO BUILD CONFIDENCE

DR. MELISSA CAUDLE

CERTIFICATE
of
COMPLETION

CONGRATULATIONS

PRESENTED TO

FOR

Writing Short Words and Sentences in Cursive

Blythe

_____   _____
DATE   SIGNATURE